Ahead of Your Time

A Complete Guide for
End-of-Life Planning

by Dick & Sue Coffin

Published by Rogan's Memorials

First printing 2006

ISBN 0-9788439-0-8

Printed in Canada
$19.95

Photo credits: ©iStockphoto.com (Betsy Dupuis, rjmiz, Arctic Flea, Rosmarie Gearhart, Slobo MITIC,
Jennifer Trenchard, Anita Patterson, Mark Strozier, Maartjie van Caspel, Stefan Klein, Sharon Dominick,
Christine Baldras, Andriei Tchernov, David Freund, Robert Kyllo, Eugenia Kim, Ahdoorubble, Mark
Strozier, Tomaz Levstek) Wendy Brown, Stephanie Paul, Pat Kelley, JGroup Advertising

Design and editorial production by JGroup Advertising
6 West Market Square, Suite 7 | Bangor, Maine
www.jgroupadvertising.com

Contents

*This book is dedicated to Priscilla Coffin,
a loving and wonderful mom.*

Ahead of Your Time

*When you are sorrowful look again in your heart,
and you shall see that in truth you are weeping
for that which has been your delight.*

~ Kahlil Gibran

We're writing this book for one reason: we want to help you understand all the benefits of preplanning end-of-life choices – for yourself or for a loved one. Why? Because, after 27 years in the monument business, we've seen too many people struggling to make difficult decisions at the hardest of times.

Although there's no substitute for sound, professional advice, we hope you'll find the information we've included in our book useful and that it will make things easier for you, your family, and your friends when the time comes.

– *Dick and Sue Coffin*

Thoughts from Dick

My wife Sue and I own a small retail monument business in Bangor, Maine. Every year, the local garden club puts on a flower show as its annual fundraiser, ushering us from the icy depths of winter to the welcoming blooms of spring. In 2000, we were invited to set up a monument display among the floral showcase. The response to our presence at the show was quite interesting, to say the least.

About half the show-goers simply walked by with little reaction. Another curious quarter stopped to ask questions, seeking information. The final quarter was upset to see us at the show. "What are *you* doing here?" they asked. Many of them slid to the far side of the aisle as soon as they spotted us – as if we had the plague.

From our experience in the monument business, we know the reactions at the flower show reflect pretty accurately how people deal with death and dying. Like the questioners at the show, only about one third of our monument business is conducted with people in a preplan situation. The other two-thirds, whether put off by fear or apathy, arrive in our shop a little lost and looking for advice. Essentially, very few people do anything about their final plans.

It's not like buying a car, a process that we go through every few years. Instead, it's an unfamiliar course of action that we don't know very much about. After all, we only die once. Maybe with a little preplanning, we can do this last thing right.

And that's the reason for the book. We want to encourage people to get their affairs in order. We want them to know why to do it and how to do it. We want to offer a simple game plan, suggesting what steps to take and what questions to ask. Ultimately, we really want to ease the burden of difficult times for our loved ones and yours.

Thoughts from Sue

Joe & Priscilla Coffin

When my mother-in-law Priscilla passed away, my husband's family arrived at the funeral home and received a packet that expressed all her wishes. I'm sure it was the nicest gift she had ever given to them. As their mom, she had taken care of business and allowed them the time to grieve. Her funeral was exactly what she wanted, her estate was in order, her grave was picked out, and her monument was already set. No second guessing for her children, no huge decisions at the hardest of times. Thank you, Priscilla, for giving us that.

One other little detail she planned (*also a good piece of advice*) was the greatest idea I had ever heard. In her will, she stated that anyone who contested her decisions would be excluded from the inheritance. So she did get exactly what she wanted. Interesting, don't you think? What a lady!

Of course, that's not our experience in the monument business. Families, ready to put closure to their loss, walk through our doors to purchase monuments. Often, every member of the group knows exactly what their loved one would want, and they are not in agreement. My heart breaks when I listen to their arguments or hear them say, "I wish this had been taken care of when he was alive." Those left behind to make decisions want the best, but they just don't know what that is.

Priscilla's preplanning was indeed a gift, a blessing really. And anybody can do it. Her example shows that if you take care of business now, you can do anything you want and leave your loved ones with harmony and peace of mind.

Keep Your Fork

Not so long ago, a lovely young woman received horrible news. Diagnosed with a terminal illness, her family doctor told her that she had only three months to live.

Always practical and efficient, she began immediately to make a preplan. She asked the parish pastor to help her get her affairs in order, to hear her final wishes. She shared with him thoughts and plans for her funeral service. After she outlined scriptures to be read, hymns to be sung, and flowers to be displayed, the pastor gave her a hug and prepared to leave.

But at that moment, the young woman suddenly became animated, and she caught the pastor by the arm. "There's one more thing," she said.

"What's that?" asked the pastor.

"Much more important than anything else we've talked about, I want to be buried with a fork in my right hand."

Dumfounded, the pastor simply stared, unsure what to say.

Laughing at his dilemma, the young woman rescued him. "Don't be surprised," she said. "I can explain. At a church social a few years ago, my grandmother whispered to me as the dishes from the main course were being cleared – 'Keep your fork.' Ever since that moment, those words have delighted me; they signal that something better is coming – like velvety chocolate cake or deep-dish apple pie. Something wonderful and extraordinary, something with substance."

– Author Unknown

Your Final Arrangements

*No one can confidently say that he will
still be living tomorrow.*
~ Euripides

for preplanners

Who will plan your final arrangements if you don't? Your spouse? Your child? Your parent? If the term loved one means anything to you, you will do everything in your power to spare family and friends unnecessary pain. Sadly, nothing will pain them more than your death. The last thing they need at such a time is the burden of making guesses and decisions about your last wishes. They need the time to grieve.

So, take final arrangements into your own hands. Make your wishes known by preplanning every aspect of your passing. From obituaries and funeral arrangements to wills and estate plans – even to the lettering and wording on your gravestone – almost every decision can be yours. And every decision you make takes the burden off others.

preplanning your funeral serves three purposes

- It allows you to make careful decisions that reflect your taste, standards, lifestyle, and budget.

- It takes the responsibility and added anxiety of decision-making from your loved ones during a difficult time and gives them a sense of peace and satisfaction because they know they've carried out your wishes.

- It reduces expenses. Often decisions made when people are upset and grieving aren't the most sound. When you preplan, you can decide exactly what you want and what you want to spend. You can even do some comparison shopping. Although you can certainly preplan without prepaying for your arrangements, some funeral homes will allow you to lock in fees at today's prices, protecting you against escalating costs and ensuring that the necessary funds have been set aside.

and if you do prepay as well as preplan, be sure to ask these questions:

- Can I change or cancel my plan?
- What happens if I relocate?
- What happens if death occurs out of state?
- What happens if the funeral home goes out of business?
- Will my funds be kept in a protected account?

Remember, preplanning helps your loved ones by taking difficult decisions off their shoulders.

To preplan for the end of your life, take the following steps…

- Compare funeral homes, legal and financial counselors, and monument providers. Gather brochures, make visits, and compare services, goods, and costs.
- Meet with professionals in every aspect of your planning. Ask questions.
- Evaluate your budget and funding options.
- Select merchandise, legal options, investment plans, and services.
- Document your plans. The forms at the end of this book will help you to record just about every plan you'll need. See form 1A (*p. 72*) to get a jump on your preplanning.

And remember that your careful preparation will only be helpful if you communicate your wishes to your closest family members and provide them with copies of your plans.

On Her Own

"The day Neal died *(September 29, 2004)* I knew I needed to buy a burial plot. So, there I was that afternoon trying to come up with more than a $1000 to buy one," explained Laurie Gildart. "If I'd had the plot ahead of time, things would have been much easier."

When Laurie Gildart's husband of twenty-five years succumbed to a brain tumor, she admits that she was unprepared to make so many decisions so quickly – and on her own. Though she knew that Neal had a living will and wanted to be buried at Mount Hope Cemetery in Bangor, Maine, virtually every other decision was hers to make at a time when, as Laurie said, "You can't really think about what you're doing. You're able to function, but it's hard to focus and think clearly."

One decision she made was to select a photo that she and Neal had taken of Mount Katahdin, the northernmost tip of the Appalachian chain, to be etched into the gravestone. She knew that Neal would approve since the mountain had been a special place for them. But few other decisions came so easily.

Professionals at the hospital where Neal spent the last few weeks of his life had given Laurie a list of signs that would prepare her for Neal's passing. Once he was gone, she wished she had another list that told her what to do next. "If we had planned ahead, I could have talked to Neal, and my decisions would have reflected his wishes too," said Laurie.

"If we had planned ahead ... things would have been much easier."

Notifying Family & Friends

*A man's dying is more the survivors'
affair than his own.*
~ Thomas Mann

for preplanners

One of the first steps your loved ones will take upon your passing is notifying others about the death. When they are already grief-stricken, such communication can be challenging and stressful. If you did not preplan, family members or friends will have to make a list of whom to call and consider what to say before they ever pick up the phone.

With preplanning, you will already have provided a list of contacts complete with phone numbers (*see form 2A on p. 75*). Though the task awaiting your family members will not be easy, your careful preparation has made it infinitely more manageable.

for family and friends

- Think about what you want to say before you pick up the phone, and you will be better prepared to deal with the emotions of the moment.

- Find a quiet, private place to make the calls.

- Speak clearly and slowly.

- Identify yourself and describe your relationship to the deceased.

- Soften the blow with a warning shot. *example:* "I'm afraid I have some bad news to share with you."

- Share the news using direct wording (*no euphemisms*) to assure understanding. *example:* "So-and-so died last night."

- Prepare yourself to answer questions about the circumstances surrounding the death.

- Keep the conversation short and focused. If necessary, use a standard line to end the call. *example:* "I'll have to say goodbye now; we have a lot more people to call."

With so many calls to complete, make the first one count. Call a close family member or friend to help you contact the people you wish to inform. If you have a preplan list from the deceased, just highlight some people for your helper to call. If no list has been prepared, you'll appreciate your friend's help with brainstorming names and following through with the calls.

Writing the Obituary

'Tis very certain the desire of life prolongs it.
~ Lord Byron

for preplanners

Once calls have been made to close family, friends, and important associates, it's time for your loved ones to turn to a broader audience. It's time to put together information to be published in your obituary. Your loved ones may find it hard to compose an accurate biography of your life, especially if the obituary writer will be one of your children. After all, your children simply weren't around for the first twenty or thirty years of your life. And how well do you think they've listened?

Who better, then, to pen your obituary than you? You *(most likely)* remember all the significant details, and you know what's important to you and how you'd like to be remembered. So, write your obituary today – and review it yearly for updates and changes *(see form 2B and the sample obituary on p. 76)*. If you find the task too intimidating, you can still preplan by listing important dates and accomplishments.

for family and friends

- Begin by identifying the deceased with a full name and tell where and when the death occurred. *(You may also choose to explain the cause of death.)*

- Follow the announcement with one or two tidbits of notable information about the deceased's life. Focus on what's most important – such as career accomplishments, charitable service, family commitment.

- Then go back to the beginning *(So-and-so was born…)* and tell a brief, but statistically detailed, chronological history of the person's life.

- List close relatives who have died before the deceased and those who have survived.

- End with specific information that tells mourners when and where services will be held. The last paragraph may also suggest where to send charitable donations.

When writing an obituary, you'll want to include special details that add interest and paint a vivid picture of your loved one. Did she grow the biggest tomatoes in the county? Did he attend the soccer games of every grandchild? Bring the deceased back to life with personal details. And don't worry about your writing skills – your funeral director and newspaper personnel have experience molding information into a well-written obituary.

Keeping Records

We understand death for the first time when
he puts his hand upon one whom we love.
                              ~ Madame de Stael

for preplanners

Once the community learns about your death, your loved ones will be inundated with calls and cards. Special friends will send food, gifts, and flowers. Though you might have been able to predict that Aunt Helen would send her famous chicken casserole, there's really no way to preplan for responses to a death.

Eventually, your family will want to contact people who expressed their concern and thank them for their support. In order for your loved ones to keep track of who did what, suggest in your preplan that they keep a notebook in a single, convenient location (*like near the phone*) for recording calls and gifts. They might collect sympathy cards in the same location (*see form 2C on p. 79*). And you can help by leaving them an accurate and complete address book.

for family and friends

If you're fortunate enough to have friends knocking at your door during this difficult time, put them to work. Talk will come more naturally when you're busy. And, with others to help, you'll have a chance to share your feelings and to get some rest. Put someone in charge of the following chores.

■ Answering the phone, screening calls, logging messages

■ Recording information gathered while making necessary calls – to places like the funeral home, the hospital, the insurance agency, the lawyer, the bank

■ Organizing sympathy cards

■ Listing gifts – like food and flowers – complete with givers' addresses

Don't count on memory to recall who sent flowers to the funeral home or church. After the service, collect every card from the arrangements, so you can thank the people who sent them. You might also make notes about any special floral displays that touched your heart.

Immediate Care of the Body

*For death is no more than a turning of us
over from time to eternity.*
~ William Penn

for preplanners

Between the time that you die and the time that you are formally put to rest, your body requires attention. Care of the body involves a number of options, depending on your wishes. How will the body be transported? Where will it go? Will organs be donated? Will the entire body be bequeathed? Will an autopsy be performed? What arrangements must be made *(see forms 2D & 2E on pp. 80 & 81)*? Clearly, your loved ones will be forced to deal with some pretty hefty questions.

That does not have to be the case, however, if you outline your decisions in a preplan. Knowing what you wanted will take a great deal of weight off the shoulders of grieving loved ones.

for family and friends

Transportation

The body will go *(if it's not already there)* to a local hospital by way of an ambulance or hearse. The doctor, the funeral director, or a family member or friend can call to make arrangements. Once death has been pronounced, the funeral director will transport the body to the funeral home to await decisions about final disposition.

Autopsy

An autopsy to determine the cause and circumstances of a death is usually not required. In about 20% of cases *(generally when the cause of death remains in question)* the coroner will require an autopsy and the state incurs the cost. Families may also request an autopsy and pay for the service themselves.

Family and friends sometimes worry about a formal viewing of the body following organ donation or an autopsy. But since both procedures are performed with surgical precision, the body is not disfigured, and an open casket for the viewing poses no problem.

Organ Donation

If the deceased is a registered organ donor, family members will be contacted by hospital personnel and asked to give permission for organ donation. Once approved, hospital personnel will make arrangements with the Organ Procurement Organization (*OPO*). The OPO checks a list of possible recipients and determines usability of organs. Then they retrieve, preserve, and transport the needed organs. The OPO, which covers the costs of all procedures, also compiles follow-up data about donors and recipients.

Body Bequeathal

Body bequeathal, which promises the donation of an entire body for scientific study to advance surgical and clinical procedures, must be arranged well in advance. Every organization that accepts cadavers for study publishes its own policies about acceptance, denial, location, and funding. When a body is bequeathed, the institution to receive the body (*most often a university*) will be notified by the deceased's family or personal representative. Following the study, the university will cremate the remains for burial in the campus cemetery or contact the family to make other arrangements.

On Borrowed Time

At 48, Tom Brown was living on borrowed time. He needed a heart transplant, and the odds were against him. In and out of the hospital and plagued by weight loss and dependence on oxygen, he was losing ground. But he never lost faith.

Seven years earlier, he had gone down while playing basketball with buddies and suffered a massive heart attack. The treatment? An experimental drug that gave him renewed energy and the semblance of a normal life. He enjoyed his work as an attorney, afternoons on the golf course, and time spent with family – his wife Gail and their three children, Win, Jill, and Greg. Weekends filled with long walks, yard work, and lobster stew seemed proof enough that life was good. But darker times lurked barely a heartbeat away.

Tom Brown with granddaughter Anya

"My gratitude to my donor and his family is matched only by my confidence in the future."

As the effectiveness of drug treatments waned, Tom developed a nagging cough and eventually ended up one midnight in the emergency room with congestive heart failure. It was the first of five hospital stays within a four-month period. In the intervals between visits, Tom's living room became a hospital zone, complete with gurney-style bed, oxygen tanks, an intercom, and emergency buzzer on the phone. He no longer had the strength for the 25-minute struggle up the stairs to bed.

Despite loving care from family and friends and a determination to beat the odds, physical complications escalated. And emotional setbacks also began to take their toll – Tom missed son Win's graduation from Bates College and daughter Jill's high school graduation. Then, in June 1989, Tom's life was on the line, and Eastern Maine Medical Center airlifted him to Brigham and Women's Hospital in Boston to await a heart transplant, his last chance.

Optimistic and hanging on to hope, Tom battled to get on the organ donation list. Down from 185 to 126 pounds, his body refused to cooperate. Inconsistent vital signs, temperature spikes, and organ malfunctions made him an unacceptable recipient. Then, though exhausted and reduced to communicating with the wiggle of a toe, the touch of a hand, or the blink of an eye, suddenly his condition stabilized. Then he and Gail had to face the most agonizing step yet – waiting for a perfect donor match. In the meantime, they learned a bleak statistic about organ donation – far more need than donors. And the situation hasn't changed much in seventeen years. In 2005, only 14,489 donors stepped forward to meet the needs of nearly 92,000 waitlisted patients needing organ transplants.

News for the Browns came in early July. A compassionate family, facing the death of their young adult son, gave life by donating his organs. During a five-hour operation, Tom received the young man's heart.

Without the gift of life made possible by organ donation, Tom would have missed a lot in the seventeen years since the transplant. Instead, he saw Win receive his master's at the Carlson School in Minnesota; he danced with Jill on her wedding day; and he and Greg shared more than a few rounds of golf. He goes to work, plays golf, has dinner with his wife, visits their seaside cottage in Georgetown as often as possible, and absolutely revels in the simple joys of being a grandpa. And, he does everything in his power to make himself worthy of the remarkable gift he was given.

Making Arrangements

We only part to meet again.
~ John Gay

for preplanners

With so many ways to celebrate your life, preplanning becomes especially important. Do you want a funeral service? A viewing? A visitation? A memorial? Will your services be public or private? Will you choose burial or cremation? It's all about your personal preferences, which may, in fact, be very different from the preferences of your loved ones.

So, how will your loved ones know, once you are gone, what you would have chosen?
The answer: you simply have to let them know *(see form 3A on p. 82)*.

as you make plans

Making choices about the final disposition of your body assumes that you know what the alternatives are. And you should know, first of all, that they're infinite. From a motorcycle brigade to a block party to mummification, anything goes. Most people, however, will follow a traditional path and select one or more of the following options.

Viewing

Sometimes known as a wake, a viewing provides a time for mourners to pay their respects by viewing the body of the deceased and to offer their condolences to family members in a less formal setting than a funeral. A viewing often precedes a funeral.

Funeral

A formal ceremony for someone who has died, a funeral honors the dead and gives mourners a chance to pay respects. Usually held at a church or a funeral home, a funeral features hymns, a eulogy, readings, prayer, and speakers extolling the virtues of the deceased.

In 1984 the Federal Trade Commission established the Funeral Rule, which imposed a few regulations on funeral providers. Essentially, the Funeral Rule requires that a funeral director must provide a consumer with an itemized list of services and merchandise. Then the consumer may select from the list, even when the funeral home offers package pricing. A preplanner, then, may also gather itemized lists from any number of funeral homes for comparison shopping.

Visitation

Like a viewing, a visitation provides a time for mourners to pay respects and offer condolences in an informal setting, but the body of the deceased is either not present or has been cremated and may be present in an urn. The visitation option can replace the need for a funeral.

Committal

Burials and cremations, two types of committal services, entrust the body's remains to a designated place for perpetual care. Sometimes a graveside service is held, and sometimes the service is held in a special place where ashes are scattered.

Memorial

A service for someone who has died, a memorial celebrates the life and accomplishments of the deceased without the body being present. Often, a memorial service is held weeks or months after the death has occurred.

Even in mourning, we celebrate
the lives of our loved ones.

Funerals, Viewings, & Visitations

*While we are mourning the loss of our friend, others
are rejoicing to meet him behind the veil.*
~ John Taylor

for preplanners

Funeral services, viewings, and visitations, all commonly held at a funeral home or church, require a great deal of planning and attention to detail. Where will services be held? Will your casket be cherry or mahogany or bronze? Do you want an open casket? If you do, what will you wear? What music will you select to be played at your service? And the list goes on.

With a preplan, you can express your personal wishes regarding services and save your family a lot of time trying to decide what to do – and trying to figure out what you would have wanted.

If no plans have been made, a loved one must start from scratch. Decisions, which often end up being guesswork under difficult circumstances, must be made quickly with little time to reflect. But a funeral director can ease the burden by leading your family members through the process with professional expertise.

for family and friends

Myth – *Prices for funeral services are uniform.*

Fact – No standard prices have been established for funeral services, so prices vary widely from one funeral home to another. It will be worth your while to compare prices by asking each home under consideration for a comprehensive, itemized list of costs.

Myth – *A body can be preserved to protect it from decomposition.*

Fact – The body begins its process of returning to the earth almost immediately. Even with the advanced technology used in today's funeral industry – embalming, waterproof caskets, sturdy vaults – nothing will preserve a body forever.

Myth – *The law requires a dead body to be embalmed.*

Fact – Embalming, a process that temporarily preserves the body, is never required for the first 24 (*often 48*) hours, and in many states it is not required at all. If a delay is necessary before final disposition of the body, refrigeration offers an acceptable alternative.

Myth – Preplanning funeral arrangements guarantees costs.

Fact – Though you will find a preplan exceptionally helpful at the time of a loss, even if the plan has been prepaid, the wise mourner should anticipate additional charges for services selected at the last minute – extra flowers, prayer books, refreshments, or other items added to the preplanner's plan.

Fact: The word funeral *finds its origins in the ancient Sanskrit word for smoke, a reference to cremation.*

Though research would suggest that the average cost of a funeral may be about $7,000 *(2005)*, preplanning can significantly reduce costs. The emotional response to your death may send grieving, ill-prepared relatives to the funeral home to prove how much they loved you by overspending on your funeral. The price-is-no-object mentality invariably escalates costs.

Asking questions and gaining industry knowledge will also help control costs. For instance, did you know that costs for opening and closing a grave vary markedly by time of day and day of the week? Excavation prices double after 3 pm while weekend costs may triple or quadruple.

Committal Services

*And meeting again, after moments or lifetimes,
is certain for those who are friends.*
~ Richard Bach

for preplanners

Like funerals, viewings, and visitations, committal services such as burials and ash scatterings – which often follow traditional funeral rites – bring up another list of questions for preplanners. Of course, the first question is about burial and cremation – which will you choose? And if you choose cremation, will you also want your ashes scattered? Most preplanners will make such basic decisions, but few will move on to consider the details of committal services.

Whether planning a burial service or a cremation service, you will need to reflect upon the available options and make selections based on personal preferences and beliefs that your family will be able to honor.

If, however, no preplanning is done, they will be left with a difficult decision between burial and cremation – and with all the details that either selection encompasses.

for family and friends

After the funeral, many families continue with their commemoration of the dead by extending services to include burials and cremations. Consider the following as you plan for committal ceremonies.

Burials

A burial service, held at the graveside, commits the body to the earth. A formal service may include music, readings, speeches, and other special features.

Laws regarding burials are looser than most people think. For instance, a burial need not take place only within a cemetery. But it's difficult to get a handle on what's allowed and what's not, for restrictions vary dramatically from one municipality to the next. If burial is the choice, you will find a number of options: in a cemetery, at sea, in outer space, even, perhaps, in your own garden. As with all your choices, consider the wishes and dignity of the deceased.

Cremations

A cremation service, held in place of a funeral or following the funeral, also deals with the body's remains. Like a burial, a formal service may include music, readings, and speeches, but unlike a burial, an especially important feature may be the scattering of ashes.

Though in our experience, we envision ashes as fireplace remnants, the ashes left following cremation are quite different. Since cremation reduces the body to its base elements, the ashes – essentially bone fragments – are rather coarse and grainy. They may be buried, kept in a cemetery vault or niche, distributed to family members in urns, or scattered in a special place.

Star Trek creator Gene Roddenberry had his ashes shot out of a rocket and scattered in space.

Scattering ashes according to a preplan makes your job easy. But what if all you know is that your loved one wanted a cremation and a scattering? Consider carefully when you select a place to scatter ashes. How will you feel if the beautiful meadow where you scattered the ashes of a loved one is developed into a bustling shopping center?

Memorial Services

God gave us memories that we might have
roses in December.
                              ~ J.M. Barrie

for preplanners

Though most preplanners will select a funeral, a visitation, or a graveside service, some will choose a memorial service to celebrate their lives in a personal and informal manner.

for family and friends

A memorial service offers a number of advantages for family and friends who wish to honor and remember a loved one. And a memorial allows you the flexibility to make decisions that will benefit everyone involved.

Time
You can choose a time that is convenient for you and for everyone you want to attend. For instance, those who need to travel long distances can take advantage of economical airline pricing, and those who hold jobs can arrange time off.

Place
Though you may follow the traditional route of selecting a funeral home or a church to hold a service, perhaps a cabin on the lake, a country club, or a fraternal lodge might be more meaningful.

Preparation
With the added time to prepare, some guests may perform a favorite piece of music or give a speech to honor the lost loved one. Others might want to read a poem or put together a video presentation. Like planning any celebration, you are bound only by your own imagination and your sense of decorum.

Invitations
Will you make phone calls, place an announcement in the local paper, or even send formal invitations?

Unlike a funeral, a memorial service does not have to be held right away. It can be held whenever and wherever you want, lessening pressure and providing time for thoughtful planning.

One popular way people inspire memory during a memorial service is to create a picture board. Photos of the deceased that span the years can be carefully arranged and highlighted with words and memorabilia to bring smiles and tears to loving viewers.

And You Wonder

The Orono High School gymnasium was filled to capacity on March 8, 2002. Coaches, ballplayers, and fans from all over Maine arrived not for a ball game, but for a memorial service to pay tribute to Joe Paul, a man who had touched their lives. Joe had spent untold hours in that gym, coaching, watching his children play, and serving as the athletic director.

Nancy Paul, Joe's wife of 42 years, explained that holding the service in the gym was a practical decision since she knew the funeral home simply wasn't large enough to hold the many mourners who would want to pay their respects. But the choice also perfectly reflected Joe's love of sport.

Joe and Nancy Paul

"You think of all the things you could do differently, but you do what you do."

Nancy was grateful for the professional and personal attention she received from the funeral providers, overwhelmed with the kind words and amusing golf tales shared by good friends, and extraordinarily proud of children Jeff, David, and Stephanie, who spoke with love about their father.

But she recognized how preplanning could have made things easier. "I've always been bothered that there was no music; there were definitely some songs that I could have chosen that had special meaning for Joe and me. It just got lost in the shuffle," she said. She also was amazed that, in the confusion, she had not thought to ask a minister friend, a man she and Joe socialized with, to preside at the service. "You think of all the things you could do differently, but you do what you do. And you wonder what he would have wanted," said Nancy.

Chapter 4

Legal Aspects

Getting Your House in Order

*Death is beautiful when seen to be a law, and not
an accident - It is as common as life.*
~ Henry David Thoreau

for preplanners

From a legal perspective, preparation for your passing presents another long list of questions. What legal action will you take during your lifetime to ensure the quality of your final days, to guarantee that your funeral wishes are honored, and to provide for your loved ones after you are gone? Questions include… What will happen if you become too ill to care for yourself? Who will inherit your property? Who will take care of your affairs after your death? As you preplan, make sure to address such important topics as advance health care directives, power of attorney, wills, probate, Medicaid, and hospice care with your legal counsel.

If you don't preplan, the consequences may be worse than you'd expect. Unless you have granted your permission, a designated loved one – even a spouse – cannot just step in to make decisions for you. Family members may argue about your care or about your things; and as they get into heated exchanges, a stranger will determine your care while the government gleefully walks away with the bulk of your savings.

as you make plans

Six important legal issues that deserve your preplanning attention…

Living Will – allows you to make decisions about your health care should you become unable to communicate your wishes

Power of Attorney – names an agent who can make legal decisions for you whether or not you are able to make them for yourself

Last Will and Testament – bequeaths your property and monetary assets as you instruct

Probate – facilitates the transfer of your property when you die

Medicaid – reduces medical costs for people unable to pay their expenses

Hospice – ensures compassionate and comfortable care for the living as death approaches

It's important to recognize that the law is always in flux. A 20-year-old can learn the requirements for a living will, income caps for estate taxes, or guidelines for Medicaid eligibility. But he can't expect the rules to be the same when he turns 40 – or even 21.

In other words, even after you do your homework regarding legal issues, you're not done. You must revisit and review regulations and policies regularly to make sure your preplan still makes sense.

The Living Will

As it is with a play, so it is with life – what matters
is not how long the acting lasts, but how good it is.
                                            ~ Seneca

for preplanners

An advance health care directive, more commonly called a living will, gives you the right to make decisions about your medical care – even after you may be too sick to communicate your wishes. But you have to plan ahead by getting a copy of the document, filling it out, signing it in the presence of two witnesses, and letting your loved ones know that you have it and where it is. Getting a sample copy of an advance health care directive is easy. You can find one online and at locations like your town office, the public library, and even the department of motor vehicles, depending on where you live. You also need to know that requirements concerning the directives fluctuate constantly and differ from state to state, so it's important to check changes in the law against the document you have prepared about every two years.

Without a living will, your loved ones will be burdened with life-and-death decisions should you become incapacitated.

as you make plans

Generally speaking, an advance health care directive form – or living will – puts your desires in writing in case you become unable to make decisions for yourself *(see form 4A on p. 92).*

Follow six basic steps to complete your living will…

- Choose someone *(your agent)* that you trust to make healthcare decisions for you if you become too sick to make them for yourself. Two witnesses must sign the advance directive that names your agent.

- Select treatments that you approve under certain situations. *(The form covers such issues as consciousness, tube feeding, pain relief, and your doctor's judgment.)* Once you indicate your preferences, your agent must follow your wishes. However, if you choose not to have CPR *(cardiopulmonary resuscitation)* if your heart or breathing stops, you'll need to take further action. You'll need to have your doctor write a Do Not Resuscitate order *(a DNR)* and place it in your medical record. You may also choose to wear a special bracelet or carry a card that indicates your preference for DNR in an emergency situation.

- Indicate whether you want to donate organs and tissue when you die. No matter what you decide, however, you may be surprised to learn that your family will make the final decision. But at least they will know what you wanted.

- Name a primary care physician or healthcare provider to determine your health care and impart his expert opinion to your agent.

- Describe your requests about your final arrangements *(funeral and burial)* or name someone to make those arrangements for you.

- Sign the form in the presence of two witnesses, who must also sign the form. At least one of the witnesses should not be a family member, and neither should be named in your will. Tell loved ones about your completion of the form and provide copies to your family members, your doctor, and the hospital. Also carry a copy with you when you travel.

Another option is to file your advance health care directive with the U.S. Living Will Registry *(www.uslivingwillregistry.com)*. Once it's electronically stored, a healthcare provider can access it twenty-four hours a day, seven days a week. Then make sure to let your family and friends and your doctor know that you have filed.

Durable Power of Attorney

Just where death is expecting you is something we cannot know; so, for your part, expect him everywhere.

~ Seneca

for preplanners

Selecting a person to take on the responsibilities of durable power of attorney is like writing a blank check. You authorize the person you choose *(agent)* to make legal decisions for you – about property, finances, and more. Your agent, for example, may use your funds to pay for your support and care, handle legal claims made against you, prepare and file your tax returns, or make charitable donations in your name *(see form 4B on p. 93)*.

When you are ready to hand over the reins or when you are incapable of making decisions for yourself, the agent you named in your preplan will step in. Remember that the agent is someone you have appointed, someone you trust and respect, someone who understands your goals and values. With few restrictions, the agent will take over and manage your daily business, acting in your best interest.

If you have not selected an agent, however, the responsibility for your care most likely falls upon a family member already trying to cope with your failing health. Even more disturbing, the court may appoint a representative that you would not have selected in a thousand years.

as you make plans

Besides keeping your wishes at the forefront, setting up durable power of attorney also saves money.

- If you sit with your lawyer to fill out a document for durable power of attorney, you will spend about $200 *(2005)* and receive four originals of the document.
- If you lose the ability to make your own decisions and have not arranged for durable power of attorney…
  - *the court will appoint a guardian to make decisions about your body*
  - *the court will appoint a conservator to make decisions about your finances*
  - *you will spend between $1500-2500 (2005) in legal fees*

Even if you and your spouse own everything jointly, both of you still need durable power of attorney. For instance, if you are incapacitated, your spouse can carry on some business as usual – writing checks and making withdrawals from savings accounts.

But both signatures are needed for quite a few transactions. Your spouse cannot change a beneficiary, sell stocks, or sell property on any joint accounts without your signature – unless you have granted durable power of attorney.

Writing a Will

*Our death is not an end if we can live on in our children
and the younger generation. For they are us, our bodies
are only wilted leaves on the tree of life.*
~ Albert Einstein

for preplanners

Statistics show that about 70% of adults avoid writing a will. Whether you find the idea too gloomy, you fear tempting fate, or you just don't think you have the time, a will is necessary if you want to be the one to make decisions about how your property will be divided. Certainly, after years of living, you have accumulated treasures and forged relationships that are important to you. In your will, an integral part of a good preplan, you can stipulate exactly how you will share your assets with those you love *(see form 4C on p. 94)*.

If you die with no will in place *(if you die intestate)*, the court will determine how your property will be distributed with no regard for your wishes. Your loved ones will be left to squabble among themselves and cultivate hard feelings though they really have no say. And, a good portion of your assets may be claimed by the state.

as you make plans

You can find books and websites to help you draft your own will. However, meeting with a lawyer provides you with professional expertise, allows you to ask questions, and ensures the document has been drawn up properly.

To be valid, a will must follow set requirements. It must be…

- made by a person 18 years old or older
- made voluntarily and without pressure
- made by a person who is of sound mind
- signed in the presence of two witnesses
- signed by the two witnesses *(not named as beneficiaries of the will)* in the presence of the person making the will
- dated on the day it is signed

Some lawyers recommend an innovative final step in the process of preparing your will – licking the envelope. With incredible advances in science so commonplace in today's world, your DNA on the seal guarantees that you – and no one but you – approved the enclosed will.

Preparing for Probate

*What is death to me? I have sown the
seeds others will reap.*
~ José Rizal

for preplanners

Another important consideration as you preplan is probate. Simply explained, probate is the legal process allowing for the transfer of property when you die. At its simplest, steps in the process include collecting all assets and property, paying outstanding debts and fees, and transferring property to heirs. Ideally, a personal representative *(called an executor/executrix in some states)* that you named in your will oversees your estate and complies with the will. The personal rep may also be called on to settle disputes if your will is contested.

If you did not appoint a personal representative or neglected to draw up a will, a court-assigned representative will take on the probate responsibilities for settling your estate. And, as you know, that means that your wishes may not be clearly understood or respected. Family members unhappy with the piece of the pie that you left them, for example, may choose to challenge your will, and they have three years to do so. A solid preplan – administered by your personal representative – will help to make your will airtight and thwart disgruntled heirs.

as you make plans

Common misconceptions about probate, based largely on past practice, often send people running in the opposite direction. The issues? Time, money, and privacy. Probate can take years to complete, especially for larger estates. Fees such as real estate and property appraisals, court expenses, and attorney's charges can cost the estate from 3-7% of its total value. Once in probate, a will becomes public record and can be viewed by anyone who cares to see it.

In purpose, though, probate exists to protect, rather than to penalize, the parties involved. In recent times it has become more friendly and informal than in the past. Usually the process runs smoothly and is over in months rather than years. Nonetheless, the probate system still remains generally misunderstood, and what people most want to know about probate is how to avoid it.

In fact, there are a number of ways to avoid the probate process completely. Since probate is connected to your will, you can avoid the process by pursuing alternative ways to bequeath your wealth.

Four primary avenues for sidestepping probate include...

■ Joint ownership of assets
When the names of two people are recorded as owners of a house, a car, a boat, and one person dies, the property automatically transfers to the other.

■ Designation of beneficiaries
On an insurance policy, a bank account, or a retirement plan, funds automatically transfer to the named beneficiary upon the owner's death.

■ Revocable/Irrevocable trusts
Assets described in a trust pass automatically to the named beneficiary upon the owner's death.

■ Gifts
Over the course of a lifetime, a person is allowed to gift others $11,000 a year without tax penalties (*2005*), capping off at a $1 million maximum.

How long does probate take? Now there's a question without a direct answer. With a well-designed preplan, the initial process may be over in a matter of days with a final date to close probate set only nine months from the time of death. But, in some instances – if the will is contested, if beneficiaries are difficult to locate, or if problems with property arise – probate may turn into a nightmare and not be settled for years. Again the advice? Preplan... and preplan well!

Medicaid Concerns

Get the coffin ready and the man won't die.
~ Chinese Proverb

for preplanners

When the elderly contemplate final plans, they often turn their attention to Medicaid. They've heard stories about exorbitant costs for long-term health care, and they fear losing their health – and then their savings – as they pay mounting bills. But they also know that Medicaid – a medical assistance program for those with limited incomes – can help. So, they seek advice about how to preserve their assets while gaining eligibility for Medicaid benefits.

But it's not as easy as it sounds. A complicated and ever-changing program, Medicaid imposes restrictions and penalties that make preplanning a challenge. The bottom line: if you fail to transfer assets before applying for Medicaid, those assets will be devoured by healthcare costs and filing penalties. On the other hand, most elder care attorneys advise their clients against transferring assets too early – when they're still healthy and independent. So it's a tough call. The constant, however, remains the same: preplanning *(though the timing may be tricky)* is the way to go.

One obstacle for preplanners is based on federal and state concerns about funding Medicaid, which in 2002 accounted for 50% of all nursing home payments. In 2005, a MetLife market survey listed the average daily rate for a stay in a nursing home at $203, or $74,095 a year. Afraid that middle and high-income elderly will try to avoid such costs by dumping their assets just to reach required poverty levels, the government regularly takes steps to discourage their efforts to qualify. In February 2006, for instance, President Bush signed the Deficit Reduction Act, which imposed a change in Medicaid's "lookback" period from three years to five. What that means is that you must apply for Medicaid benefits five years *(the "lookback" period)* before you think you'll need them. During that five years, you must limit transfers of funds and property to specific allowable circumstances in order to retain eligibility.

If you are in the position to request Medicaid relief, you have a number of options that will allow you to avoid forfeiting your savings in order to qualify. To gain eligibility, you must have no more than $8,000 in cash and investments, excluding your house and its furnishings, personal belongings, your car, and a mortuary trust. In addition, a healthy spouse is allowed a $99,540 exemption.

Medicaid regulations change yearly, so you will want to update your knowledge regularly about restrictions both at the federal and state levels. You may also want to contact a trusted attorney who specializes in elder care matters and to express your wishes to a loved one.

as you make plans

Medicaid imposes exacting restrictions about disposing of assets to gain eligibility. It does, however, allow the transfer of funds and property in select situations.

You may transfer funds to…

- a spouse
- a blind or disabled child
- a trust for a blind or disabled child
- a trust for a disabled adult under 65

You may transfer your home to…

- a spouse
- a blind or disabled child under 21
- a disabled adult under 65
- a sibling with equity in the home who has resided with you for at least one year prior to your institutionalization
- a child who has lived with you for at least two years prior to your institutionalization and who has provided health care allowing you to stay at home rather than in a nursing home

As people age and consider issues like long-term health care, they worry that they'll need to sell their homes to pay mounting bills. In fact, such fears are truly unjustified.

Statistics suggest that most of us will not spend time in a nursing care facility. Even if we do, the time will be brief: over 50% of nursing home stays last six months or less and only 10% of patients remain institutionalized for more than three years. With good financial preplanning *(which you'll read about in chapter 5)*, you'll have the funds to cover healthcare costs even if you're one of the few to end up in a long-term care facility. And your home will be safe.

End-of-Life Care

*The day which we fear as our last is
but the birthday of eternity.*
                        ~ Seneca

for preplanners

Before you find yourself at death's door, take a closer look at your advance health care directive. Whether you completed a living will or named a guardian with medical power of attorney, you should determine exactly what you want for end-of-life care. Do you hope to die in an institution or at home? What measures do you find acceptable for sustaining your life? What procedures do you approve to ease your pain? In essence, how prepared are you to die? One way to respond to such questions with informed answers is by connecting with a hospice care program *(see form 4D on p. 95)*.

Hospice care *(and palliative care)* organizations specialize in end-of-life services. With the primary goal of ensuring death with dignity, hospice provides care for the patient and the entire family through a team-oriented method. A doctor, a nurse, a social worker, a counselor or religious guide, and a trained volunteer will work with you and your family – as often as possible in a home setting – to manage your care if you become terminally ill. Rather than attempting a cure, hospice and palliative care manage your symptoms and take steps to alleviate your pain, keeping you comfortable during your final days.

You must be proactive in your preplanning, or your loved ones will find themselves forced to be reactive. And their reactions – keeping you hooked to life-support machines or overmedicating you with pain killers – may not be what you wanted at all.

Most people say that they hope to die in their own homes – and when they're ancient and fast asleep. National studies report that such wishes are not the reality. Only about 25% of people die at home despite the statistic that shows over 80% would prefer to die there.

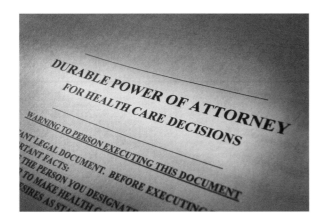

as you make plans

Hospice workers are powerful advocates who can ensure the quality of your end-of-life care. But it's important for you to be your own advocate long before the time comes. More detailed information about the inner workings of hospice will help as you decide whether to pursue such care. To help with your decision, consider the following...

■ Advance health care directives are frequently challenged and ignored.
  Find ways to put some teeth into your plans.
  – *Select a spokesperson with a backbone.*
  – *Explain your plans to family members who might object to your decisions.*
  – *Discuss your wishes with your physician.*
  – *Make sure your physician is willing to honor your requests.*
  – *Put your plan in writing.*

■ Medicare does cover hospice care.

■ Though self-contained hospice facilities exist and are becoming more common,
  you can receive care at home, at a nursing home, and even in a hospital.

■ Pain can be effectively and safely alleviated to keep patients comfortable.

■ Hospice care can begin within 48 hours of a doctor's referral.

■ Hospice nurses are prepared to respond to emergency calls 24 hours a day, seven days a week.

■ Hospice programs are licensed by the state and regulated by the federal government.

Broken Promises

Even multimillionaires, who have managers and advisors to oversee their affairs, sometimes get caught with no plans. Such was the case for Barry White – perhaps the world's most famous bass crooner of sexy love songs. He died of kidney failure in 2003.

White, married for twenty years to his second wife and former back-up singer Glodean Davis, never drafted a will. Before he died, the two had been separated for several years, and he lived with Katherine Denton (*another former back-up singer*) and their one-year-old daughter Barianna in an exclusive gated community in Los Angeles.

Even the rich and famous neglect estate planning, subjecting their families and partners to bitter feuds.

So... when Barry White died at 58, no plans were in place to settle his estate. Estranged wife Glodean was named administrator. And paramour Katherine Denton, who lawyers claim White referred to as his fiancée, filed suit against the estate. Later, Denton offered to drop the suit and future claims in exchange for the $2 million home she said that White had promised her. Glodean refused to negotiate.

And that's only part of the story. Other women came forward with paternity suits, hoping to claim a bit of White's fortune. Loved by millions, Barry White will have women wrangling over *his millions* for years to come.

White joins other notables – *Abraham Lincoln, Conrad Hilton, Jimi Hendrix, Howard Hughes, and Pablo Picasso* – who died without wills in place.

Sharing Your Financial Plans

*That man is successful who has lived well,
laughed often, and loved much.*
~ Robert Louis Stevenson

for preplanners

From a fiscal perspective, your death will trigger all kinds of activity. And the more you preplanned, the more will be left in your estate to be shared with your heirs. Consult a financial advisor to learn how to protect your assets by making annual gifts, by capping out your lifetime gift tax exemption, or by making direct payments on a child's tuition and medical bills. Investigate such topics as insurances, division of assets, trusts, and estate taxes.

Who will know what your estate entails and how you wish to allocate your property after you die? The responsibility for settling your estate will be overwhelming for a loved one grieving your loss, especially if taking on the assignment suddenly. A preplan will better prepare your named agent to handle your affairs.

as you make plans

If you've worked with a financial advisor, you probably have developed a promising fiscal outlook. Now, just add a personal element by sharing a record of your assets with an important person in your life (*see form 5A on p. 96*).

- Record all your assets in a notebook or on a piece of paper and keep it in a safe place.

- List bank accounts, insurance policies, retirement plans, real estate, stock holdings, antiques – even money under the mattress!

- Ask a relative or friend to act for you when you die. Choose someone who thinks like you, someone you trust.

- Meet once a year with that spokesperson to discuss your financial wishes, to explain changes in your plan, to look over the documents, and to indicate where records are kept.

People are surprised to learn that a will does not supersede other documents. For that reason, it is important to keep your designation of beneficiaries up to date on all your policies. If you stated in your will, for example, that Uncle Henry will inherit the funds from an insurance policy, but Aunt Martha is named as the beneficiary on the insurance document, Uncle Henry is out of luck (*unless he is very kind to Aunt Martha*).

Considering Life Insurance

And in today already walks tomorrow.
~ Samuel Taylor Coleridge

for preplanners

One of the first questions to ask yourself is, "Do I need life insurance?" If you have no minor or adult dependents, your answer may well be "No." But the answer usually isn't that easy. Even if you know your answer is "Yes," you're left with more questions – Why do I need it? What should it do for me? What kind of insurance is best for me? Spend some time considering your circumstances and researching your options. Insurance plans like term, permanent, whole life, universal, and variable – a narrow sampling of insurances available for you to purchase – offer different features to meet your needs.

As you preplan, you may want to sit with an insurance agent or a financial planner to discuss your long-term and short-term goals and devise a plan that works best for you. If you make no conscious decision about life insurance, however, you may overlook an excellent way to provide for your loved ones.

as you make plans

A life insurance option can provide significant benefits…

Cash at Death – Life insurance policies are payable immediately upon death, which can be useful to pay funeral expenses and debts.

No Probate – Since the proceeds from life insurance are not subject to probate, you can collect without cost or delay.

Death Tax Reduction – A life insurance payout is not considered part of your estate and therefore will not be included among your taxable assets.

To be an informed life insurance consumer, you'll want to compare companies, rates, and other features for various policy types. An easy way to research is online. Try www.selectquote.com and www.iquote.com. Then call an agent or a broker for personal service.

Providing for Your Minor Children

*Let children walk with Nature... and they will learn that
death is stingless indeed, and as beautiful as life.*
~ John Muir

for preplanners

As you make your will, plan your funeral, establish a trust, and make countless other plans, don't forget to plan for your greatest asset of all – your children. Who will provide for them – financially and emotionally – once you are gone? Since most parents name each other to inherit the estate, the children remain unprotected in the unlikely event that you and your spouse die together. As secondary beneficiaries, young children will be unprepared to manage for themselves.

How can you preplan so that you guarantee a secure future for your children?

as you make plans

Financial planners suggest several ways to safeguard your children…

Establish a Trust

A trust names a trustee to act on behalf of your child until the age you have specified is reached. The trustee follows your instructions and files income tax returns.

Name a Property Guardian

You can name a person in your will to oversee property for a minor child, and the court will follow your wishes when the time comes.

Name a Custodian

Another way to appoint a manager for property you wish to leave to your child is through the Uniform Transfer to Minors Act. Named in your will or living trust, the custodian manages the property until your child becomes an adult.

While financial support for your children is important, emotional support is a far greater concern. Careful consideration must be given to naming a guardian for your children. And the best advice is to name a single guardian *(rather than a couple – who might split up)* and an alternate.

Some questions to ask yourself: Who loves my children? Who shares my beliefs? Whom do I trust without reservation? How will my children respond to a new home, new parents, new siblings? Who has the time, the physical ability, and the resources to care for my children?

Naming Beneficiaries

I'm not afraid of death. It's the stake one puts up
in order to play the game of life.

~ Jean Giraudoux

for preplanners

More than likely, you have named beneficiaries on any number of documents and in your will or trust. But did you know that naming a beneficiary – even when you have not written a will – serves as an automatic and immediate death benefit? Now that you are preplanning, you may want to consider taking advantage of pay-on-death *(POD)* and transfer-on-death *(TOD)* accounts. Since they avoid probate, POD and TOD accounts pay beneficiaries directly following a death – and without fees. It would be a good idea to check every policy, document, and account you have signed and to inquire about survivor benefits.

With all the paperwork you encounter in your life, designation of beneficiaries can easily become haphazard and outdated. A good preplan sets aside time to update your documents. You might, for instance, recheck every policy, document, and account early in January to make sure that you are satisfied with the beneficiaries you have named.

as you make plans

Bypassing the will, pay-on-death and transfer-on-death beneficiaries skip the probate process, so they transfer immediately upon your death. They also incur no attorney fees, court costs, or appraisal charges. You can name POD and TOD beneficiaries on quite a number of your holdings…

- Bank accounts
- Insurance documents
- Stocks
- Bonds
- Money markets
- Retirement plans
- Automobiles

Check with your financial advisor to get and fill out the necessary forms for this easy transfer of your holdings.

One word of advice about POD and TOD accounts: keep your beneficiaries up to date!

Do you really want proceeds from your insurance policy to go to your ex-spouse? What good does it do to transfer the money in your bank account to your father – when he died ten years ago? Updating your designation of beneficiaries is truly a gift that allows you to take care of the ones you most love.

Establishing a Trust

To live in hearts we leave behind is not to die.
~ Thomas Campbell

for preplanners

You may want to set up a revocable trust to shelter your assets, especially if they are significant (*$2 million or more*). A revocable trust, also known as a living trust, involves a grantor, a trustee, and a beneficiary. During your lifetime, you will fill all three roles and retain total control. Considered part of your estate and subject to taxation during your lifetime, a revocable trust may be altered or terminated to meet your needs.

Once you die, the trust becomes irrevocable and a trustee you have named will follow your instructions about distributing property, paying taxes, and providing for your heirs.

A trust isn't for everyone. If it's not in your preplan, that probably is fine. On the other hand, if you have significant holdings, your heirs stand to lose a sizable portion of your estate unless you protect them by setting up a trust.

as you make plans

Why a trust and not just a will?

- You retain control for as long as you live. A revocable trust is known as a living trust, so it's dynamic and changing, not just a pile of papers in a safe.

- You have the authority to name another person to oversee your affairs should you become incapable of making decisions for yourself. And you can change that designation at any time.

- You can provide for minor children or other beneficiaries who may not be able to manage their own finances – with specific, detailed instructions.

- Your heirs avoid the expense and delays of probate court; proceeds from a trust fall directly into their hands.

- You reduce estate taxes for your heirs because the funds set aside in the trust are sheltered from taxation upon your death.

Do not presume that establishing a trust negates your need for a will. You should draft a will in conjunction with your trust and any other preplanning strategies that you undertake.

Covering Funeral Expenses

Until death, it is all life.
~ Miguel de Cervantes

for preplanners

Few people are ready to take on significant financial burdens suddenly thrust upon them when there's a death in the family. Even when a death is expected, expenses can be prohibitive. How will your loved ones fare when you die? Will they be forced to wipe out a savings account? Will they rack up over $5000 of debt on a high-interest credit card? Or… have you taken responsibility for finances in your preplan?

If you're the type who likes to have control, you may decide to keep funds in your own hands and transfer them to your beneficiaries at death. If that's your plan, let your loved ones know where you have set up the account and that the funds have been targeted to pay your funeral expenses.

as you make plans

To cover your funeral expenses, you might consider a Totten Trust, a simple payable-on-death vehicle for saving money. The Totten Trust has a number of clear-cut advantages…

- ■ You can set one up through your bank using an easy, straightforward form.

- ■ You avoid joint ownership. Since your beneficiary has no access to your account, your assets remain safe.

- ■ You avoid the expense and delays of probate court, so your beneficiary can use the money immediately following your death to pay for funeral expenses.

- ■ You reduce estate taxes for your heirs.

- ■ You retain control for as long as you live.

A simple savings account that is payable-on-death, a Totten Trust is set up through your bank, though not through the trust department, which makes the process easy. Since it does not require a written trust agreement, it incurs no attorney's fees. *(Costs for other kinds of revocable trusts will vary depending on your holdings and your bank or lawyer, but a typical bill ranges from $2,000 to $3,500.)* Your bank will set up a Totten Trust account for you at no charge.

A Mortuary Trust

Death never takes the wise man by surprise;
he is always ready to go.
                    ~ Jean de La Fontaine

for preplanners

Though some people are comfortable taking charge – like those setting up Totten Trusts to cover funeral expenses – others prefer to put the details and paperwork in someone else's hands.

One preplan tactic relies on professionals to set up and administer a mortuary trust to prepay funeral costs. With a mortuary trust, an individual *(the payor)* provides the funding and signs a binding legal contract with a funeral home. The contract requires the funeral home, acting like a trustee, to set up a formal savings arrangement through a bank or credit union to cover the funeral expenses of a named beneficiary *(not necessarily the payor)*.

To sidestep possible drawbacks of prepayment, check into the reputation of the home, learn the penalties for cancellation, and understand inflation expenses. Find out what will happen to your funds if the funeral home goes out of business.

as you make plans

To choose a mortuary trust that's right for you, look into two options...

Credit for Services
This type of mortuary trust does not specify exactly which services will be provided by the funeral home. Instead, it uses the funds deposited into the trust *(and the accrued interest)* to pay for funeral costs when the time comes.

Guaranteed Price
If the payor prefers to stipulate services, a detailed document is prepared that selects funeral items like a casket, a liner, an urn. Based on the theory that interest gained in a mortuary trust will match inflation rates, the prices paid up front can be "guaranteed" even though they're bound to increase over the years. And if items become unavailable, the contract states that a similar product of equal or better value will be substituted.

All this and tax help too! A mortuary trust can be set up as a qualified funeral trust *(QFT)*. If a payor restricts contributions to allowable limits *($8,200 for 2005)* for QFT eligibility, the funeral home takes over tax obligations. A representative from the home will withdraw necessary funds from the mortuary trust to pay income taxes on the trust's earnings to the IRS. At the same time, the payor is not required to report the interest as income when filing an individual tax return.

Estate Taxes

*There are always death and taxes; however,
death doesn't get worse every year.*
                              ~ Author Unknown

for preplanners

Most of us will never be worried about paying a huge estate tax. On the other hand, quite a few families will establish estates worth at least $1.5 million. Those are the people that need to know about estate taxes. And what they will learn is scary!

Essentially, if you die wealthy, the federal government will assess a tax on your heirs that will take 45% of every dollar *(beyond the tax-free $1.5 million)* that you have left them. The percentage jumps to 47% for a $2 million estate. And the pattern continues: the higher your tax bracket, the higher the taxation percentage.

But there's good news. The federal government intends to abolish estate taxes completely by 2010. The scheduled plan gradually changes the tax-free amounts from $1.5 million in 2005 to $3.5 million in 2009. And the next year is free and clear.

as you make plans

To protect your investments – so you can leave as much of your estate as possible to loved ones – you should investigate ways to shelter your assets from taxation. Ask your financial advisor about a(n)...

Bypass Trust – and how investing an amount equal to the current maximum tax exemption *($1.5 million in 2005)* into a trust upon the death of your spouse doubles your allowable exemption.

QTIP Trust – and putting an amount equal to the current maximum tax exemption *($1.5 million in 2005)* into your spouse's trust while you retain the right to name the beneficiary.

AB Trust – and how a surviving spouse can stay financially comfortable when the partner's half of the property is earmarked for children or beneficiaries other than the spouse, thus reducing the spouse's estate and tax obligations. Then, once both parents are gone, it's possible that the maximum amount *($3 million in 2005)* may have been saved for the children.

Roth IRA – and converting a regular IRA into a Roth account, which can reduce estate taxes and eliminate account income taxes for your heirs.

Never believe that a plan proposed by Uncle Sam is a done deal. In 2010, when a Congressional tax plan calls for the end of estate taxation, Congress may decide that the United States simply cannot afford to repeal all estate taxes. So, rather than counting on a vague promise, you may want to take other avenues to protect your assets from excessive taxation.

Better Late Than Never

When 75-year-old Albert Foster announced to friends that he was ready to retire, he simply meant that he'd spent enough time at work. He certainly was not ready.

Though he had established a successful pharmacy in Machias, Maine, and lived comfortably and amiably in the small coastal community, he had done absolutely no financial planning. He had not even applied for social security.

In stepped Joe Coffin, a financial planner, who just happened to be Albert's good friend and brother-in-law. In no time, they put together a plan. They filled out the paperwork for social security and put the store on the market. Before long, Albert had received a tidy sum from Uncle Sam and collected a small fortune for the business, the building, and the inventory.

Proving that it's never too late to make a plan, Albert followed Joe's advice and invested all his assets in a portfolio of high-yield growth securities. Then he and his wife Marion retired to their summer cottage on the coast to relax and watch rose-colored sunsets. And all the while, their portfolio grew.

Chapter 6

Commemorating the Loss

A Final Resting Place

*Memory is a way of holding onto the things you love,
the things you are, the things you never want to lose.*
~ from *The Wonder Years*

for preplanners

Many of us feel great comfort when we visit a loved one's final resting place. We can plant flowers, trace the engravings on a monument, speak aloud our thoughts, our worries, our hopes. It is the perpetual memory of a life too short – and it will be there long after we and our children and our children's children are gone.

Options are growing and changing, but basic choices include selecting a cemetery, purchasing a burial plot, deciding on a gravestone, and designing that gravestone. It's a matter of forever. What do you want forever to say about you? A solid preplan will include such eternal decisions.

Without a preplan in place, choosing a burial spot and a monument become the responsibility of your loved ones. And by now they're overwhelmed with all the decisions you didn't make. So preplan now.

Often people associate perpetual care with the actual physical care of the gravesite, and they worry about regular cleaning and care of the stone. But their worries are foundless. Gravestones have survived hundreds – even thousands – of years. And granite? It's simply indestructible. The only maintenance that a gravesite needs is the care performed routinely by cemetery personnel – like mowing the grass. So, finally, there's one thing you don't need to plan.

as you make plans

What should you know about preparing your final resting place?

Cemetery selection
You'll need to look into your choices. Do you want to be buried where you live now? Where you lived then? Where your parents or children live? Find out which cemeteries are open and which are closed, learn about religious affiliations, visit plots for sale, and ask about resident vs. non-resident fees.

Purchasing a plot
Plots come in different sizes and allow for single or multiple burials. Fees range widely, depending on size, location, and residency. For a standard single plot, you might pay $100 in Acme, Arizona, but $1600 in Forest Park, Illinois.

Gravestone choice
Granite, which comes in a variety of colors, is the most popular choice for grave markers and monuments, but you can also choose marble and bronze. A monument provider will show you samples of all three, both in foot markers and upright monuments. Again, costs fluctuate depending on what you want, but an average granite grave marker should cost around $500.

Gravestone design
Besides the engraved lettering of names, dates, and simple epitaphs, monument providers can offer hundreds of other options: etching, sand-blasting, vases, emblems, ceramic photos, borders and edges, finishes, and custom designs.

Selecting a Lot

We should all be concerned about the future because we will have to spend the rest of our lives there.
~ Charles F. Kettering

for preplanners

If you have thought about selecting your final resting place, you know how hard it can be.

Do you have a picture in your mind of your gravesite? Can you envision every detail? Or do you have no clue whatsoever? Take some time to drive around to cemeteries, get out and wander the grounds, note features that you like.

Then talk with family members about your plans and theirs. Compare all the towns where you've lived and determine which you'll claim for eternity. Consider how family traditions *(both sides for married couples)* play into your selection. Before you decide, you'll probably go back and forth, uncertain of the best choice. If that's the case, then how can you possibly expect your loved ones to make the decision for you? Let them know what you want *(see form 6A on p. 98)*.

as you make plans

Like every step in the process, choosing a cemetery lot requires your thought. Some of the questions you might ask yourself are…

- Which cemeteries support my religious beliefs?
- How many burials/markers are allowed per lot?
- How convenient will it be for loved ones to visit me there?
- What setting is most important to me?
    - *sunny or shady?*
    - *by a river, a garden, a tree?*
    - *with a majestic view?*
    - *facing east or facing west?*
    - *near the roadside?*

No matter the answers, preplanning provides the time to give careful consideration to your perpetual care.

The price of a cemetery plot covers the cost of the land and a fee for maintenance. But it's not legally a purchase of real estate – it's a binding lease. Even so, you should treat it as property by securing a deed and marking the corners of the property under the direction of the cemetery sexton. *(You can purchase decorative makers from a monument company.)* That way, you'll make sure that people who own the adjoining plots will not encroach on your property, and your plot will have room for more burials if needed.

Your Gravesite

*May the road rise up to meet you, may the wind be ever at your back. May
the sun shine warm upon your face and the rain fall softly on your fields.
And until we meet again, may God hold you in the hollow of his hand.*

~ Irish Blessing

for preplanners

From simple grave markers to showy mausoleums, the choices for identifying your final resting place
vary greatly. The look, the stone, the design, the cost – as well as family considerations and local
customs – all come into play. Occasionally, the deceased or the family of the deceased wants to make
unusual arrangements. They may select a columbarium, a niched wall for keeping urns. Or they may
want to build a mausoleum, a large, stately tomb. Most often, the choice comes down to grave markers
and monuments.

What your family wants, however, should remain secondary. What do *you* want? If you don't choose
the simple grave marker that expresses your no-nonsense nature, you just may end up entombed in a
costly, ornate mausoleum. Or vice versa.

as you make plans

Though grave markers and monuments are the most common choices, you can choose from a variety
of options for indicating your grave.

Grave Marker
Also called a footstone, a grave marker is set flush into the ground and generally marks the grave
of an individual.

Monument
A monument is a two-piece structure consisting of a base and a die. The die, which displays the lettering
and design elements, rests on the base. Using epoxy, the two pieces are attached and set on the burial plot.

Mausoleum
An above-ground building that serves as a tomb, usually for at least two family members, a mausoleum
requires extra maintenance from the cemetery crew. For that reason, most cemeteries ask families who
build mausoleums to establish a trust with the cemetery and the municipality in which it's located.

Lawn Crypt

A smaller version of a mausoleum, a lawn crypt, which entombs two bodies, is built partially underground and supports a grassy surface.

Columbarium

A columbarium, an existing feature in most cemeteries, is a wall with recessed chambers suitable for holding funeral urns.

As you decide what will work best for you, be creative. It's not necessarily an either-or situation. A common practice used by many families is to mark the family plot with a monument engraved with the last name and to use separate grave markers for each family member buried on the site.

And even if you hope your ashes will be kept by a loved one or scattered in a special place, you still may want to purchase a grave marker or monument. A spot in a quiet cemetery dedicated to the deceased invites loved ones to visit the site for prayer and reflection. Removed from the hubbub of everyday life, it offers a peaceful place to make personal and spiritual connections.

The term *mausoleum* comes from the name of an ancient Mediterranean king, Mausolus. When the king died in 353 BC, his forlorn wife Artimisia honored him by building a spectacular marble tomb. She commissioned leading Greek artists to design the tomb and had it constructed high atop a hill overlooking the city of Halicarnassus. Stone lions and mounted warriors guarded the massive structure, which boasted 36 columns and depictions of Greek myths. At the very top, Mausolus and Artimisia rode in a colossal chariot pulled by four magnificent steeds. The tomb, named as one of the Seven Wonders of the Ancient World, stood for centuries until 1404 AD when it was ravaged by earthquakes.

The Monument Provider

Don't cry because it's over. Smile because it happened.

~ Dr. Seuss

for preplanners

Like funeral directors, people in the monument trade know the value of putting their clients at ease. They expect that their customers will have limited knowledge about the purchase they're about to make – and that's okay.

Your monument provider will encourage you to ask tons of questions and offer ideas, pointing out that almost anything is possible. They may suggest taking pictures or finding illustrations or images. Then when it's time to sit down with your monument experts, you'll have a sense of what you want, and they'll know how to help you. A little imagination, coupled with boundless versatility in design and lettering, will lead to a satisfying choice *(see form 6B on p. 99)*.

Once again, if you avoid taking care of this detail in advance, others will struggle to guess what you may have wanted.

as you make plans

Professionals in the monument business believe that the advantages of making decisions before death are significant…

- You can compare providers – expecting a monument professional to…
  - *record information to go on the stone (family name, first and middle initial, maiden name, date of birth, date of death)*
  - *suggest design options and inspirational words for the epitaph*
  - *check with the cemetery sexton to learn expected protocol and correct placement of stones*
  - *perform required foundation work*
  - *transport stones to the cemetery*
  - *position stones on the plot*
  - *match stones and/or lettering with ones already existing on the plot*
  - *inspect the condition of an existing stone before cutting a second name or date*

- Without the urgency of an imminent burial, there's time to shop, to do homework, to find a monument business that offers excellent service.
- You can take the time to get exactly what you want – the perfect plot, gravestone, and design.
- You'll be more likely to select merchandise that you can afford.

Most monument companies today have computer software that will let you sit down with an expert to design a headstone or other marker. You can select materials, lettering, special treatments – like etchings and sandblasting – and see the results on a computer printout. And you can try as many different designs as you want before you make your final decision.

Once you select a design and check it carefully for correct dates and spellings, your monument expert will electronically send the document to the plotter for application to the stone. This foolproof process assures that you get exactly what you approved.

It's even possible – if you're a great preplanner – to place your stone on the plot long before you die.

Making Special Plans for Veterans

*This nation will remain the land of the free only so long
as it is the home of the brave.*
~ Elmer Davis

for preplanners

In recognition of service to their country, veterans are entitled to a free grave marker – a death benefit that will require some preplanning. The US Veterans Administration oversees the process for obtaining the marker, which is relatively simple, but the requirements are specific and well defined. If you're a veteran making an end-of-life preplan, you're in the perfect position to select the marker you prefer, provide accurate information for engraving, and communicate your wishes to your monument provider as part of your planning.

Your loved ones will understand the magnitude of your service to your country. And they'll want to do the right thing if arrangements are left to them. But will they know what "the right thing" is?

for family and friends

If you're faced with making arrangements for a veteran, getting information from the Veterans Administration will be helpful. They can tell you about...

■ Eligibility – Five categories of eligibility allow for free grave markers. *(But each category has detailed regulations that you can review to determine whether the deceased meets required standards.)*
  - *veterans and members of the armed services*
    (must die on active duty or receive discharge other than dishonorable)
  - *reservists*
  - *commissioned officers of the NOAA*
  - *commissioned officers of public health service*
  - *WWII merchant marines*

For their sacrifice, the United States honors our veterans with free burial in a veterans' cemetery. While every veteran is entitled to this excellent benefit, thought is needed before plans are made. That's because most veterans' cemeteries are regional, which may make visiting the gravesite inconvenient – even a burden – for family members and loved ones. In Idaho, for instance, the only veterans' cemetery is in Boise. From Port Falls, in the neck of the state, a family would have to make a seven-hour trip to visit the gravesite. And that's just one way!

■ **Markers** – A veteran may choose from three common grave markers.
   – *flat marker in granite, marble, or bronze*
   – *upright monument in granite or marble*
   – *niche markers for cremated remains kept in a columbarium*

■ **Inscriptions** – Headstones and markers furnished by the government must be inscribed in English with the following information, in the order presented.
   – *legal name of the deceased*
   – *branch of service*
   – *years of birth and death*

If space is available, the inscription may also contain the veteran's rank, war service, military decorations, awards, and month and day of birth and death.

Ordering
Markers may be ordered from the Veterans Administration by any person handling the affairs – not necessarily a relative.

Applications
You can obtain an Application for Standard Government Headstone or Marker by writing to…

     Monument Service
     Department of Memorial Affairs
     Veterans Administration
     941 N. Capitol St., N.E.
     Room 9320
     Washington, DC 20420

Finding Closure

People do not die for us immediately, but remain bathed in a sort
of aura of life... It is as though they were traveling abroad.

~ Marcel Proust

for preplanners

Once the immediate activity of a death has passed, your loved ones will have time to mourn more quietly, to find their own special closure. And there's no preplan for that.

Some sense of peace may come as they respond to people who sent cards and gifts. Then when they sort through your personal belongings, they will continue to experience the loss in very personal ways. They may decide that some special remembrance must be created in order to gain a comfortable sense of closure.

for family and friends

A visit to the cemetery will offer comfort and a way of remembering. But a remembrance can have even greater power with a bit of time and imagination. Consider the following ways to honor a life important to you.

Gift – Making a donation to the deceased's favorite charity or special organization is a thoughtful gesture that would meet with your loved one's approval. Gifting may also be a preplanner's choice, often replacing flowers at a funeral.

Foundation – Through donations, you can set up a foundation in your loved one's name that will benefit others for years to come. For instance, a scholarship for a nursing student may be set up by a family who has lost a dedicated, career nurse. Setting up a foundation may also be a preplanner's choice with a request for donations, instead of funeral flowers, written into the obituary.

Book – A book, whether publishable or more like a scrapbook, provides a remembrance that can be saved and shared with others.

Video – A video DVD captures not only the words and images of the deceased, but favorite places, interests, and music. It can also include especially touching tributes from family and friends.

Place – You might dedicate a garden outside the door or plant a tree in the backyard to remember a loved one.

Object – A baseball preserved on the mantle, a wooden spoon hanging in the kitchen, an old rocking chair on the porch – choose a special item that will recall memories of a loved one.

Setting up a foundation is no easy task. That's why you'll want to turn the work over to a mutual fund company. And you'll need at least $10,000 to create the foundation. Then, you can continue to contribute *(in $1,000 increments)* to the fund, which will grow without imposing taxes. Best of all, you can name the foundation and select the recipients who will benefit from your charitable gifts.

Not Forgotten

On Memorial Day 2006, Nicole (Nikki) Downes wanted to sit with her grandfather and share some memories. But there was nowhere to go.

You see, her grampy had passed away in October. Though the family had carried out his plans for cremation, his ashes had never been scattered or buried. As Nikki said, "He is waiting in my mom's closet for my grandmother." The plan? When her grandmother dies, Nikki and her mom will mix the couple's ashes and scatter them over the homestead the two shared for almost 50 years. And once they're at rest – in peace together – the whole family will find closure.

In the meantime, Nikki talked with her mom about her longing to spend some reflective time with her granddad. He was gone, but not forgotten. After some discussion, they decided to mark a stone for both Grampy and Grammie and place it on a family plot in a nearby cemetery. What Nikki and her mom recognized is that monuments represent the lives of loved ones and give family and friends a place to go to be with them. And Nikki was comforted by the idea of placing flowers at the grave and visiting on special occasions.

Pleased that a stone now reminds everyone about her grandparents' life here on earth, Nikki said, "It brings me great relief to have a place where I can go at any time to talk with my grampy."

Etched in Stone

Epitaphs that grace tombstones tell some fantastic tales. From ancient times to modern, the deceased often had the last word. Will some parting sentiments make their way into your preplan?

The immortal bard William Shakespeare, who reportedly died on his birthday April 23, 1616, left a warning on his tombstone. Fearful of grave robbers, he is thought to have composed the following epitaph:

Good friend, for Jesus' sake forbear
To dig the dust enclosed here.
Blest be the man that spares these stones,
But curst be he that moves my bones.

In more modern times, a woman from Olympia, Washington, who loved shopping, engraved a Visa card on the monument she shared with her husband. Then she inscribed the words,

> *Charge It*
> *Send the Bill to Heaven*

And apparently Doctor Fred Roberts of Arkansas was not about to let death close his practice, for patients visiting his gravesite read,

> *Office Upstairs*

A Latin music lover, E. Lariz, left a tribute on her Key West, Florida, gravestone:

> *Devoted Fan of Singer Julio Iglesias*

But the most well-known Key West epitaph belongs to a locally famous hypochondriac, B. Pearl Roberts, who proclaimed,

> *I told you I was sick.*

Acknowledgments

We could not have written this book without calling on the expertise of a number of professionals who gave generously of their time and thoroughly answered every question we had, no matter how insignificant.

Thank you to…

> **Joel Dearborn**, LTD, attorney at law
> Joel A. Dearborn Law Offices
> Brewer, ME
>
> **Joseph Kiley**, funeral director
> Kiley Funeral Home, Inc.
> Brewer, ME
>
> **Kandyce Powell**, executive director
> Maine Hospice Council
> Augusta, ME
>
> **Jane Skelton**, attorney at law
> Skelton Law Offices
> Bangor, ME
>
> **Marion Syversen**, financial advisor
> Norumbega Financial
> Hampden, ME

And the stories you read – they're real. We appreciate the time people spent talking openly about their personal lives – their struggles, their losses, their victories. Each one helped to illustrate the point of the book – preplanning makes a world of difference.

Thank you to…

> Tom and Gail Brown, Joe Coffin, Laurie Gildart, Nancy Paul, and Nicole Downes

Glossary

Agent The person named to take on the responsibilities required by durable power of attorney is called the agent.

Assets Land, buildings, vehicles, and other property of value, including monetary funds, constitute the assets that a person accumulates over a lifetime.

Autopsy The medical examination of a dead body, an autopsy determines the cause and circumstances of death.

Beneficiary The person named in a will, a trust, an insurance policy, or other official document, a beneficiary inherits money or property.

Body Bequeathal Body bequeathal involves a person's donation of his/her entire body upon death for the purposes of medical and scientific research.

Burial A burial is a solemn ceremony where a dead body is usually put into the ground or into the sea.

Casket A casket, or coffin, is a box *(generally decorative)* into which a body is placed before burial or cremation.

Cemetery A cemetery encompasses an area of land for burial of the dead.

Columbarium A niched wall or chamber, a columbarium displays urns filled with burial ashes.

Committal Burials and cremations, two types of committal services, entrust the body's remains to a designated place for perpetual care.

Conservator Responsible for a person who is incompetent or incapable of making decisions, a conservator makes the decisions necessary to protect the person's financial interests.

Cremation During a cremation, a dead body is incinerated until it is reduced to ashes.

Deceased The *deceased* is a way to refer to someone who has died.

Disposition Refers to the disposal of a dead body, with the most common methods of disposition being burial and cremation.

DNA The acronym for deoxyribonucleic acid found in the chromosomes, DNA carries genetic information.

Embalming A procedure used in the funeral industry, embalming replaces fluids in a dead body with preservatives that retard the process of decay.

Epitaph An inscription on a gravestone, an epitaph offers words of wisdom, a joke, a prayer, a philosophy.

Estate A person's estate includes real estate property, personal possessions, and all financial holdings.

Etching A cut design, an etching decorates a monument or grave marker.

Executor Designated in a will or assigned by the court, the executor of an estate, also called the personal representative, carries out the instructions put forth in a will.

. . . .

Final Arrangements Primarily the plans for a funeral, final arrangements may also include drafting a will, establishing a financial plan for heirs, prewriting an obituary, planning a cremation, and selecting a burial plot and monument.

Financial Planner A professional investment advisor, a financial planner assists a person with decisions about such monetary issues as insurances, investment accounts, beneficiaries, trusts, and taxes.

Foundation Established with endowment funds, a foundation offers support through charitable donations.

Funeral A funeral is a ceremony that honors the dead and gives mourners a chance to pay respects.

Funeral Director Commonly called an undertaker or a mortician and generally the owner of the funeral home, a funeral director arranges funerals and prepares the body for its final disposition.

Funeral Home A building where the business of preparing a body for burial or cremation takes place, a funeral home is also a place where mourners attend a funeral service, a viewing of the body, or a memorial.

Grave Marker A grave marker is a stone set flush with the ground that identifies the person buried or commemorated on that spot.

Guardian Also known as an agent, a guardian makes decisions about a person's body when that person is unable to make such decisions. A guardian could also be the person selected to care for children in the event of their parents' deaths.

Heir As a legal inheritor, an heir takes ownership of another's property following that person's death.

Hospice Care Compassionate end-of-life care, hospice draws on a team approach to provide comfort and dignity for both the terminally ill patient and the family.

Intestate When a person dies without a will in place, he is said, by law, to have died intestate, and the government will determine how his assets will be handled.

Lawn Crypt Featuring a grassy covering, a lawn crypt is a subterranean building that serves as a tomb holding two caskets.

Life Insurance A common way of providing a legacy for beneficiaries, life insurance plans grow during a person's lifetime with regular, monthly payments to a protected fund.

Living Will A living will states that a person does not want to be kept alive by artificial means – medications or life support equipment – when an incurable or irreversible condition exists and there's no reasonable expectation of recovery. The living will is also known as a health care advance directive.

Mausoleum Also known as a crypt or burial chamber, a mausoleum is an ornately decorated building used to house coffins.

Medicaid A program funded by state and federal coffers, Medicaid pays a part or all of the medical costs for people unable to afford medical treatment.

Memorial A service for someone who has died, a memorial celebrates the life and accomplishments of the deceased without the body being present.

Mourner A mourner is a person who grieves the loss of someone who has died.

Monument A monument is a two-piece stone that sits upright on a grave and is engraved with the name or names of the persons buried there.

Niche An architectural recess in a cemetery wall, a niche may hold a funeral urn filled with the ashes of a cremated body.

Obituary A brief written biography, an obituary outlines important information about a person's life and appears in newspapers immediately following the person's death.

Organ Donation Managed by the Organ Procurement Organization, organ donation allows a person to donate organs and tissue upon death.

Pallbearer A pallbearer is a person selected by the grieving family who will help to carry or accompany a casket at a funeral or burial.

Palliative Care Also referred to as comfort care, palliative care seeks to provide quality of life for a terminally ill patient by easing pain and suffering.

Perpetual Care Arrangements for perpetual care include selection of a cemetery plot and a monument and a design for the monument.

Personal Representative Also known as the executor or executrix, the personal representative named by the deceased handles the probate duties of the deceased.

Power of Attorney The power of attorney grants a person the legal authority to act on another's behalf concerning legal and business issues.

Predeceased Common terminology in an obituary, the predeceased are close relatives who have died before the person for whom the obituary is written.

Preplan A preplan outlines decisions about the details surrounding a death, from notifying family and friends to funeral concerns to perpetual care. Preplanning makes the wishes of the deceased clear and removes the burden of decision-making from loved ones. A preplanner may either work alone or with professionals – a funeral director, a lawyer, a financial advisor, a monument expert – to create a plan and put it into writing.

Probate The legal process allowing for the transfer of property following death, probate ensures that a will is genuine and valid.

Roth IRA A retirement savings plan, the Roth IRA boasts a unique benefit: tax-free earnings for its owner and beneficiaries who meet specific requirements. Though no deductions are allowed for contributions, the savings at the other end – when no taxes are assessed on withdrawals – more than make up for it.

Sandblasting A process used to mark a monument or footstone, sandblasting uses a pressurized jet of air and sand to clean, polish, or apply design.

Sexton A cemetery caretaker, a sexton performs such duties as bell-ringing, grave-digging, and gravesite management.

. . . .

Survivor A term used in an obituary, a survivor is a close relative of the deceased who is still living.

Trust A trust is a legal arrangement for handling finances in which a person appoints a trustee to control and manage his money and property according to the person's wishes, usually following the person's death.

Trustee The person named to control and manage a trust is a trustee.

Urn An urn is an ornamental sealed vase where a person's ashes are kept following cremation.

Vault Usually located underground, a vault is a burial chamber.

Veteran A veteran is a person who has served in the armed forces.

Viewing Sometimes known as a wake, a viewing provides a time for mourners to pay their respects by viewing the body of the deceased and to offer their condolences to family members in a less formal setting than a funeral.

Visitation Like a viewing, a visitation provides a time for mourners to pay respects and offer condolences in an informal setting, but the body of the deceased is either not present or has been cremated.

Will An official legal document, a will states how a person's property will be distributed following the person's death.

Witness A witness is a person who signs a legal document to show that he or she observed its signing by another person and that the signature is genuine.

Forms

Dear family and friends,

Now that I am gone, please read the following forms that share with you decisions I've made about my final arrangements. I hope that having an outline of my wishes will make this time easier for you.

I prepared these documents on _____.

(date)

_____

(signed)

Form 1A
personal information

About me

Legal Name _____

first, middle, last, suffix, maiden

Date of Birth _____ / _____ / _____   Gender: Male Female

Place of Birth _____

city, county, state/province, country

Residence _____

street address, city, county, state/province, zip, country

Occupation _____

Social Security Number _____ – _____ – _____   Marital Status _____

Citizenship _____

Ancestry _____

Ethnic/Race Identity _____

Religion _____

About my family

Spouse _____
       name   *years married*   *living (Y/N)*

Father _____
       name

       _____
       address

Mother _____
       name

       _____
       address

Child _____
       name

       _____
       address

Child _____
       name

       _____
       address

Sibling _____
       name

       _____
       address

Sibling _____
       name

       _____
       address

Grandchildren _____
              names

       _____

. . . .

My Contacts

Person in charge of funeral arrangements

_____
name   *phone*

Doctor _____
          name   *phone*

Lawyer_____
          name/firm   *phone*

Executor of Estate _____
                    name   *phone*

Safe Deposit Box _____
          institution name / location of key   *phone*

Location of Important Documents

Will _____   Bank Account Passbooks_____

Living Will_____   Life Insurance Policies_____

Organ Donor Card _____   Investment Documents _____

Birth Certificate _____   Income Tax Returns _____

Marriage License _____   Certificate of Ownership for Burial Plot _____

Social Security Card _____   _____

Military Discharge Papers _____   Bills To Be Paid _____

Citizenship Papers_____   Other Financial Information _____

Deeds/Titles to Property _____   _____

_____   _____

. . . .

Form 2A
people to notify

Here is a list of people who should be informed that I have died.

name	relationship	phone

name	relationship	phone

name	relationship	phone

name	relationship	phone

Doctor ——
                                                                    phone

Lawyer——
                                                                    phone

Funeral Director ————————————————————————————————————
                                                                    phone

Insurance Agent ——————————————————————————————————————
                                                                    phone

Investment Broker——————————————————————————————————————
                                                                    phone

Work Contact ———————————————————————————————————————
                                                                    phone

Additional Family & Friends ————————————————————————————————

. . . .

Form 2B
information for my obituary

Please use the following information and fill in the gaps as you write my obituary. Supply this form or a final copy to the following newspapers _____

Announcement of Death

Name of deceased _____ Date _____

City /State _____

Age_____Cause *(optional)* _____

Biography

Date of Birth _____ / ___ / _____ Place of Birth _____

Education _____

Occupation _____

Honors_____

Accomplishments _____

Military Service _____

Organizations/Charities_____

Hobbies/Interests_____

Personality Traits_____

. . . .

Predeceased by

Spouse _____

Children _____

Grandchildren _____

Parents _____

Siblings _____

In-Laws _____

Friends _____

Survived by

Spouse _____

Children _____

Grandchildren _____

Parents _____

Siblings _____

In-Laws _____

Friends _____

Services

Wake _____   Funeral _____   Graveside _____
      date/time   *date/time*   *date/time*

_____   _____   _____
      location   *location*   *location*

_____   _____   _____
      address   *address*   *address*

_____   _____   _____

Contributions

Name of Organization _____
                                                                        phone

Arrangements

Name of Funeral Home _____
                                                                        phone

Photograph Provided ☐ Yes ☐ No

. . . .

sample obituary

Carolyn "Carrie" Ryan Sewall, 92

EDGECOMB - Carolyn Sewall, 92, died Friday, October 14, 2005 at Miles Memorial Hospital in Damariscotta.

A contributor to *Audubon Magazine*, Carrie was a noted authority on owl populations in Maine and a dedicated conservationist. In 1976, she joined National Audubon Society and Defenders of Wildlife and was active in petitioning for protection of endangered East Coast bird species.

Born November 26, 1912, in Edgecomb, Maine, the daughter of James and Margaret Sewall, Carrie spent her youth reading every book she could get her hands on and riding horseback. She graduated salutatorian of the Class of 1929 at Lincoln Academy in Newcastle. And in 1933, she graduated summa cum laude from Boston College.

Following her heart, Carrie moved to Thompson Island in Boston Harbor, where she served as an administrative secretary at the Boston Farm & Trade School *(later Thompson Academy)* from 1931-1975. Besides her secretarial duties, Carrie filled in as nurse, friend, and second mother to thousands of boys who attended school on the island. She married Raymond Sewall, the school's assistant headmaster and three-sport coach, in 1936; and they immersed themselves wholeheartedly into the life of the school.

Carrie enjoyed bird watching, indoor gardening, reading, and crossword puzzles. And she never tired of learning. Not one to settle for the status quo, Carrie got her first driver's license at 82 and learned to use a computer at 88. An extraordinary communicator, sending cards and letters on a daily basis *(including 300 Christmas cards with personal notes every year)*, she championed the lost art of correspondence.

She was a member of the National Audubon Society, Edgecomb Historical Society, Lincoln County Animal Shelter, Edgecomb Cemetery Committee, and the Edgecomb Extension.

She was predeceased by her husband of 63 years, Raymond Sewall, who died in 2000.

She is survived by a son, James R. Sewall and his wife Daisy of Orono, and by her sister Lola Bragg of Amherst, Massachusetts.

A time of visitation will be held from 4-6 pm on Wednesday, October 19 at Simmons, Harrington & Hall Funeral Home, 975 Wiscasset Road, Boothbay. Burial will be in Highland Cemetery in Edgecomb at a later date.

Contributions may be made in Carrie's memory to

> Lincoln County Animal Shelter
> Edgecomb, Maine

Form 2C
gifts record

Place this sheet near the phone and use it to keep track of calls and gifts that arrive.

---

name   *gift*

---

description

---

name   *gift*

---

description

---

name   *gift*

---

description

---

name   *gift*

---

description

---

name   *gift*

---

description

Form 2D
care of my body

I have thought carefully about how I want my body treated; please honor my wishes.

I have a living will ☐ Yes   ☐ No

I want my organs donated ☐ Yes   ☐ No

List of Organs and Tissue for Donation _____

_____

Final Disposition: burial, entombment, cremation, donation to medical science *(please circle one)*

_____
location   *phone*

_____
address   *other*

Care of Ashes: *I would like my ashes… (buried, entombed or placed in a niche at a cemetery; buried elsewhere; left with surviors; scattered; other)*

_____

_____

I have also made decisions about…

Embalming ☐ Yes   ☐ No

Autopsy ☐ Yes   ☐ No

DNA Sample ☐ Yes   ☐ No

Form 2E
organ & tissue donation

I have chosen to donate life. Please honor my wishes as indicated on these forms.

Signed on _____

date

Witnessed by

_____

name

_____

name

After completing this page, make a photocopy, cut out the bottom form and keep it in your wallet. Then let your family and friends know you've done so.

DONATE LIFE   FAMILY NOTIFICATION FORM

Dear Family,

I want you to know about my decision to become an organ, eye and tissue donor. Upon my death, if I am a candidate for donation, I ask that you honor my wishes. It is important to me that others are given the opportunity to live full and productive lives.

I wish to donate the following:

☐ any needed organs and tissue

☐ only the following organs and tissue:

_____

Thank you for honoring my commitment to donate Life through organ, eye and tissue donation.

Donor Name   _____

Donor Signature _____ Date _____

MY COMMITMENT TO DONATE LIFE UNIFORM DONOR CARD

I _____, have spoken to my family about organ and tissue donation. I wish to donate the following:

☐ any needed organs and tissue

☐ only the following organs and tissue:_____

_____

The following people have witnessed my commitment to be a donor.

Donor
Signature _____ Date_____

Witness _____

Witness _____

. . . .

Form 3A
service arrangements

After my death, I would like to have the following services…

☐ viewing   ☐ visitation   ☐ funeral   ☐ burial   ☐ cremation   ☐ memorial

On the following pages (81-90), I have outlined my wishes based on the services I've chosen.

Viewings, Visitation & Funeral Services

Location _____
       name   *phone*

_____
       address

Director _____
       name   *phone*

Type   ☐ private   ☐ public

Person Presiding   ☐ religious leader   ☐ family member   ☐ friend

Casket Selection _____
       manufacturer, model name, model #

_____
       type of wood, bronze, copper, steel (16, 18, 20 gauge), other

_____
       interior material (crepe, linen, velour, velvet)

_____
       lid style (half couch, full couch)

Open Casket   ☐ Yes   ☐ No

· ·

Clothing Selections _____
          outfit/suit

          _____
          jewelry

          _____
          shoes

Music Selections _____
      title   *artist*

      _____
      title   *artist*

      _____
      title   *artist*

Organist _____
    name   *phone*

Vocalist _____
    name   *phone*

Instrumentalist _____
    name   *phone*

Readings _____
    title   *author*

    _____
    title   *author*

Readers _____
    name   *phone*

    _____
    name   *phone*

. . . .

Flowers _____
       florist   *phone*

Floral Selection 1_____

Floral Selection 2_____

Floral Selection 3_____

Floral Selection 4_____

I would like to have ☐ a guest register   ☐ thank-you cards   ☐ prayer books   ☐ memorial flyers

Memorial Displays _____
          photo display, video, awards/honors

Pallbearer _____
       name   *phone*

Pallbearer _____
       name   *phone*

Pallbearer _____
       name   *phone*

Pallbearer _____
       name   *phone*

Pallbearer _____
       name   *phone*

Pallbearer _____
       name   *phone*

· ·

Transportation for…

My body ☐ funeral coach ☐ funeral van

Family members ☐ limousine ☐ sedan ☐ self

I would like an escort

_____

police, firefighters, fraternal organization, bagpiper

Other Special Instructions_____

_____

_____

After-service Reception

_____

location   *phone*

_____

address

. . . .

Burial

Location _____
        cemetery

_____
        address

Type ☐ private ☐ public   Person Presiding ☐ clergy ☐ family member ☐ friend

Outer Burial Container _____
        manufacturer

        _____
        model name   *model #*

        _____
        grave box or liner (concrete, wood)

        Vault ☐ bronze ☐ copper ☐ plastic ☐ wood ☐ composite

        Lawn Crypt ☐ concrete ☐ wood

Music Selections _____
        title   *artist*

        _____
        title   *artist*

        _____
        title   *artist*

Vocalist _____
        name   *phone*

Instrumentalist _____
        name   *phone*

Readings _____
        title   *author*

        _____
        title   *author*

Readers _____
      name   *phone*

_____
      name   *phone*

Flowers _____
     florist   *phone*

Floral Selection 1_____

Floral Selection 2_____

Floral Selection 3_____

Floral Selection 4_____

Special Instructions_____

_____

_____

• •

Scattering Ceremony

Location _____

_____
address

More Specific Location _____
garden, burial plot, niche, other space

Funeral Director _____
name   *phone*

Type ☐ private ☐ public   Person Presiding ☐ clergy ☐ family member ☐ friend

Urn Selection _____
manufacturer, model name, model #

_____
type of material: bronze, copper, marble, wood, other

Music Selections _____
title   *artist*

_____
title   *artist*

_____
title   *artist*

Vocalist _____
name   *phone*

Instrumentalist _____
name   *phone*

· ·

Readings _____
         title   *author*

_____
         title   *author*

_____
         title   *author*

Readers _____
         name   *phone*

_____
         name   *phone*

_____
         name   *phone*

Flowers _____
         florist   *phone*

Floral Selection 1_____

Floral Selection 2_____

Floral Selection 3_____

Floral Selection 4_____

Special Instructions_____

_____

· ·

Memorial

Location _____
           cemetery

           _____
           address

Funeral Director _____
                   name   *phone*

Type ☐ private ☐ public   Refreshments ☐ food ☐ drink

Person Presiding ☐ clergy ☐ family member ☐ friend

Music Selections _____
                   title   *artist*

                   _____
                   title   *artist*

                   _____
                   title   *artist*

                   _____
                   title   *artist*

Organist _____
           name   *phone*

Vocalist _____
           name   *phone*

Instrumentalist _____
                  name   *phone*

· ·

Readings _____
    title   *author*

_____
    title   *author*

_____
    title   *author*

Readers _____
    name   *phone*

_____
    name   *phone*

_____
    name   *phone*

Flowers _____
    florist   *phone*

Floral Selection 1_____

Floral Selection 2_____

Floral Selection 3_____

Floral Selection 4_____

Memorial Displays_____

Special Instructions_____

. . . .

Form 4A
the living will

☐ *I have secured an advance health care directive from the state and have filled it out so that you will know how I wish to be cared for should I become unable to care for myself. You can find this document here*_____.

☐ *I have not secured an advance health care directive, so the following section lets you know how I wish to be cared for should I become unable to care for myself.*

I have chosen_____ to make health care decisions for me.

_____
relationship   *location*

When agent can make decisions for me _____

End-of-Life Choices

☐ Yes ☐ No I want to be kept alive as long as possible within the limits of generally accepted health care standards.

☐ Yes ☐ No I do not want to be kept alive if I have an illness that will not get better, that cannot be cured, or that will result in my death quite soon – OR – I am no longer aware (unconscious), and it is very likely that I will never be conscious again – OR – My doctor determines that the likely risks and burdens of treatment would be more than the expected benefits.

☐ Yes ☐ No I want to be kept alive with any treatment that is generally given for my medical condition even if I no longer recognize most people or communicate and understand due to serious disease or damage to my brain, even if the treatment will not cure or improve my mental condition.

☐ Yes ☐ No I want artificial nutrition and hydration regardless of my condition and regardless of the choices I have communicated about keeping me alive.

☐ Yes ☐ No I want treatment for relief of pain or discomfort to be given at all times, even if it shortens the time until my death or makes me drowsy, unconscious, or unable to do other things.

☐ Yes ☐ No Organ Donation

Primary Health Care Provider _____

Person to make final arrangements for me _____

My signature _____

Form 4B
durable power of attorney

I have selected _____ to serve as my personal representative.

_____
address   city/state

If I become unable to manage my affairs, I give my agent the power to take on the following duties...

_____   sell, mortgage, lease real estate and land   _____   buy, sell personal property

_____   control bank and personal finances   _____   control business finances

_____   manage estate and trust   _____   represent me in claims and litigation

_____   manage my retirement plan   _____   prepare my tax return

_____   contribute to charities   _____   provide for my family's needs

Other specific duties to be performed by my agent _____

Limitations imposed on my agent_____

Signatures

Mine _____

Agent_____

Witness _____

Witness _____

Date_____

Form 4C
last will & testament

Following is an excellent, barebones form for providing information that I can use to draft my will.

Legal Name _____
gender

_____
address   *city*   *state*

_____
marital status   *# of children*

Do you want to provide for children you might have or adopt in the future? ☐ Yes ☐ No

List specific gifts of cash _____

_____

List specific bequests_____

_____

Name a guardian for children _____

List primary heirs _____

List secondary heirs_____

List alternate heirs_____

Name personal representative _____

Describe wishes for disposition of remains_____

Optional Actions _____
disinherit a person, forgive a debt, name someone to care for a pet

_____

_____

· ·

Form 4D
hospice care

Should I be unable to express my wishes for end-of-life care, please follow my plans for hospice care as outlined below.

Hospice Organization _____

phone

_____

address   *city*   *state*

_____

contact person

I would prefer to die…

____   at home

____   in the hospital

____   at a nursing home

____   at a hospice care facility

I approve the following procedures for end-of-life care…

_____

_____

_____

I want hospice workers to manage my pain as needed to make me comfortable. ☐ Yes ☐ No

. . . .

Form 5A
record of assets

To the best of my knowledge, all of my assets are listed here.

Bank Accounts

_____
institution

_____
account #

_____
beneficiary

Insurance Policies

_____
institution

_____
account #

_____
beneficiary

Investment Accounts

_____
company

_____
account #

_____
beneficiary

Bank Accounts

_____
institution

_____
account #

_____
beneficiary

Insurance Policies

_____
institution

_____
account #

_____
beneficiary

Investment Accounts

_____
company

_____
account #

_____
beneficiary

Safe Deposit Box _____
            institution   *account #*

_____
contents

Real Estate

_____
property

_____
deed location

_____
beneficiary

Automobiles/Boats

_____
make/model/year

_____
title

_____
beneficiary

Real Estate

_____
property

_____
deed location

_____
beneficiary

Automobiles/Boats

_____
make/model/year

_____
title

_____
beneficiary

Significant Personal Property

Description of Item _____
beneficiary

Description of Item _____
beneficiary

Description of Item _____
beneficiary

Description of Item _____
beneficiary

Description of Item _____
beneficiary

. . . .

Form 6A
the burial plot

Please note the pertinent information concerning the arrangements I have made for my burial.

Name of Cemetery _____

_____
address   *city /state*

Location of Plot _____

Name of Cemetery Sexton_____
                                                phone

Where Title Is Kept _____

· ·

Form 6B
monument selection

I've made the following arrangements with my monument provider concerning my gravestone.

Monument Provider _____
                                                                                            phone

Manufacturer_____
                                                        model name   *model #*

Type ☐ grave marker ☐ monument ☐ lawn crypt ☐ columbarium ☐ mausoleum

Material for grave marker or monument ☐ bronze ☐ granite ☐ marble

Material for lawn crypt ☐ concrete ☐ wood

Engraving ☐ name ☐ date ☐ sentiment ☐ design

Special Instructions_____

_____

_____

Sources

Websites...

cem.va.gov

cremation.com

donatelife.net

efmoody.com

estate.findlaw.com

fcamaine.org

ftc.gov

funeralplan.com

funeral-help.com

funeralswithlove.com

funeralwise.com

growthhouse.org

kff.org

lawdepot.com

lifegift.org

medicaidhelper.com

mrestateplan.com

nationalcremationsociety.com

nhpco.org

organdonor.gov

quotegarden.com

Website articles...

Estate Planning. askmerrill.ml.com

Get Your Financial Affairs in Order. nolo.com

How to set up your own charitable foundation. suntimes.com

Myths vs. Facts. wrtc.org

Will You Owe Estate Taxes? smartmoney.com

You're Dead, Now What? forbes.com

Print articles...

Consumer Protection and End of Life Care.
Maine Hospice Council, Inc.

Dealing with Death. Mainebiz; 12 December 2005.

Funeral & Estate Planning.
Bangor Daily News; 9 March 2006.

Health Care Advance Directives: Your Right To Choose.
Bureau of Elder and Adult Services; Department of
Human Services; Augusta, ME

Disclaimer

Dick and Sue Coffin wrote *Ahead of Your Time* as a service. They want to provide a way for people to get their affairs in order, to prepare for their final days.

JGroup Advertising, in an effort to provide accurate and useful information about preplanning, conducted research for *Ahead of Your Time* from June 2005 to April 2006.

Neither the Coffins nor JGroup Advertising claims expertise, and they do not assume legal liability or responsibility for the content of the book. Please contact professionals to answer your questions about funeral, financial, and legal planning.

Dear Reader,

We hope you found our book useful – and that you're well on your way to preplanning. Remember: It's never too late to start!

But, now we'd like you to take some time to share your ideas with us. Though *Ahead of Your Time* is the first book we've written, it won't be the last. Doing some preplanning of our own, we intend to publish another edition based on your suggestions and stories.

So… we'd like to hear from you.

Name _____ Phone or email *(optional)* _____

I am a ☐ preplanner ☐ family member making arrangements for a loved one

What information in the book is most useful?

_____

What additional information should we include next time?

_____

What good preplanning advice do you have to share?

_____

Thanks for taking time to fill out this form. Now just tear the page from the book, fold and secure it, and drop it in the mail. Or…if you have a story about preplanning – or what happens when a loved one doesn't – please share it. Whether it's sad, touching, funny, unusual, or enlightening, we want to hear what you have to say. Please write us at *Ahead of Your Time*, 458 Ohio Street, Bangor, Maine 04401 or visit our website at www.aheadofyourtime.net to send your thoughts or pre-planning stories electronically.

Someday, you just may see your story in print.

Dick and Sue Coffin, *Ahead of Your Time*

I give my permission for Ahead of Your Time *to use my name, photograph, and written or spoken words in all forms in subsequent editions of* Ahead of Your Time *and in all forms and media for publicity, advertising, or any other lawful purposes. I waive my rights to inspect or approve the finished version(s).*

Signature _____ *Date* _____

Address _____

BUSINESS REPLY MAIL
FIRST-CLASS MAIL PERMIT NO. 101 BANGOR ME

POSTAGE WILL BE PAID BY ADDRESSEE

Rogan's Memorials
458 Ohio St
Bangor ME 04401-9907